CONTENTS

STEP 1: PERSONAL BRANDING

Personal branding is not about selling. It is the way other people see you. Believe it or not, you can shape these perceptions. Notice I did not say control. Shaping perception means you are mindful of how you communicate. As part of this process, you need to consider how to express who you are in writing and with visuals. It would help if you thought specifically of your audience when making those decisions.

Remember, hiring managers and recruiters will see your LinkedIn profile and quickly determine if you might be a good fit for their organization, internship, or job opportunity -- within seconds. You will not have a second chance to make a first impression. In many cases, that quick look could be your only chance with the hiring manager, and you want to make sure the impression is good.

While you cannot control what another person thinks, you can create a favorable impression. To do this, you need to know who you are, what you want, and how to present yourself in writing and visually. To do this, you will need to understand and use the different features of the platform.

Research indicates almost ninety-three percent of the meaning another person has about a person relates to non-verbal cues. Ninety-three percent!

For digital communication channels, like LinkedIn, how we write, the words we choose, the information we share all communicate non-verbally. What are you saying with your non-verbal communication? Are you enthusiastic, happy, positive? Do you give the impression of being organized and detailed oriented? Does your profile reflect your creativity?

You are a brand. How you present yourself on LinkedIn and across all digital platforms contributes to building a digital presence — a brand called "you."

As you begin to look for internships and jobs, you will need to decide what you want to do and consciously shape the person people will read about and see in their feeds.

Personal branding is an ongoing process of developing and maintaining your reputation. It is a form of self-packaging. When you go food shopping, do you ever look at the packaging? Of course, you do! Have you ever chosen bottled water because of the packaging? I know I have, even though water is water regardless of the package. What makes one brand more attractive than another? The packaging!!!! Certain packaging will appeal more to some people than it will to other people. We do not get upset because our friend prefers a different bottle shape. Do we? I certainly hope not.

The same is true of people. We tend to like people who are like us and who like us. At birth, we have the potential to be anything or anyone we can dream. As we get older, we learn what we are good at and what we like. By setting and working toward goals and carefully constructing our profiles by strategically thinking about what is important to us and what we are passionate about, we increase the likelihood of finding a position we will enjoy.

Your "brand" is what another person thinks of when he or she hears your name. It's everything others think they know about you—both factual and emotional. Your brand exists objectively, in someone's mind. These perceptions are quite powerful because our perception is our reality.

If you do not actively shape your brand, others will do it for you. It might feel a little uncomfortable to market yourself, but the reality is you are already marketing yourself. You just might not realize it.

You have the opportunity to highlight your best qualities and skills. No one knows what you've accomplished, overcome, or achieved better than you. And it is up to you to share your best self with potential employers.

At this point, you might be wondering, how do I do this?

I am going to give you an exercise to complete before you start building your profile. Answer the question: What do you want your life to look like at age 40?

Take out a piece of paper and write down where you want to live, whether you own your own home, how much money you would like to make, whether you are married or have children. Then identify a career or profession that can support your version of your best life. Please spend some time thinking about it.

Do you like working with people? Are you technically inclined? Would you prefer working as a member of a team or independently? Your personality traits matter in your job search. Take them into consideration as you begin this journey.

Next, think about how you can get from where you are now to that ideal. To set a goal and move toward it, you need to break it down into actionable steps.

Next question: What do you need to do by your 30th birthday to be where you want to be at 40? Then, think about where you want to be at 30.

You can start planning and setting personal and professional goals for the next five, ten, or twenty years. If you do not consciously make these decisions and act, you very well might find yourself at 40 years old wondering what happened.

The Conference Board reports that 53 percent of Americans are currently unhappy at work. Think about that. Over half of all people working are presently unhappy. You don't want to be one of those people, do you? I know I don't want you to be one of them.

While I can't promise the next few chapters will bring you a lifetime of career bliss, it might be able to help you avoid some of the mistakes many people make as they enter the job market.

Get Clear On Your Goals

The first thing you need to do is get very clear on the type of work you don't want to do. If you do not like meeting new people, customer service-oriented jobs will most likely not be a good fit. If you hate sitting behind a computer, graphic design or video editing will not satisfy you. Once you are clear on what you do not want to do, start thinking about what work you might like to do.

To narrow this down, research potential careers. A good strategy is to talk to people who are already doing what you want to do. Ask them questions about their typical workday.

Does it sound like something you would enjoy? Once you've narrowed it down, start thinking about internships.

For example, let's say you have the dream of becoming a broadcast journalist. If you were my student, I would encourage you to complete at least one if not two internships working in a newsroom. For many careers, you do not learn about the demands of the day-to-day in the classroom, no matter how brilliant your college professors.

A book cannot capture the nuances and demands of a job – only experience can do that. On more than one occasion, I've had students change career goals after an internship. The reality of the day-to-day grind in a particular career may not be what you think it is.

There are sacrifices required for many careers - especially when you are starting. The reality of long hours, terrible shifts, low pay, potential relocation to remote areas of the country are only a few of the realities of particular industries. Please don't misunderstand. Hard work and sacrifice are no reason not to pursue a specific career, but you need to recognize what is involved.

As a current college student or recent graduate, one thing you can do right now is to start thinking about gaining valuable work experiences to set you on the right path. After you write down your goals, we need to look at *actions* you can take to get you there, which brings us to internships.

Internships

An internship is a structured work experience to help you learn about an industry, a job role, or a business. You earn college credits and, in some cases, a paycheck.

Finding an internship will depend on a variety of factors. The most obvious, but often overlooked is access. Where is your college or university located? If you attend college in a city, internship opportunities are more easily accessible, more common, and typically more competitive.

Your approach to finding, applying for, and obtaining an internship will be slightly different from students who attend colleges in remote locations or areas of the state where there might not be many opportunities to work with Fortune 100 or 1,00 organizations.

If your college is near a train station, you might have access to a large city. For you, it is easier to find valuable work opportunities because there are more of them. The best internships are typically at larger organizations, but not always. Research indicates that over 50% of all internships lead to full-time positions - this is more likely to happen if you intern at a larger organization where there is the *possibility* of full-time employment.

In small to medium size companies, a full-time position might not be a possible next step. However, it can provide you with valuable work experience. My advice is to be aware of what the internship can and cannot do for your future. There are limitations to any internship. Use your best judgment when applying and accepting a position.

Whatever you do, please do not throw away this opportunity to learn and grow.

The National Association of Colleges and Universities reports a little over half (56.1%) of internships convert to full-time jobs. Out of desperation and a lack of planning, students accept internships that do not have the possibility of full-time employment. Don't make this mistake.

I wish I could tell you the minute you have your diploma, employers will come knocking at your door. In the overwhelming majority of cases, they will not. You will need to pursue the job and career you want. In many instances, it starts with a quality internship.

Please do your future self a favor, don't get caught up in just settling for something because it is more comfortable in the short term. I know this process might seem overwhelming. But, take a deep breath. You can do it.

Building your "brand" and online professional presence is hard work, but think of it this way, either you put in the time now or waste months, maybe years floating around unhappy because you didn't take the time to think about what you want. Not what your parents want or your teachers want, but what YOU want.

Not all internships are created equal. Sometimes you will work with people who do not value you as much as you would like or are not sure how to make your internship experience valuable. The best internships are structured. You know what to expect before you start working, and your employer has a plan for your internship work.

Unfortunately, this is not always the case. It would help if you asked these questions *before* you take the internship.

We've all heard stories about friends who had an internship consisting of making coffee or copies - this is a real possibility depending on the industry. There is nothing wrong with making copies or asking a co-worker if you can grab them a cup of coffee. However, your internship should also include work related to the position you would like to acquire after graduation.

Paid Internships

Paid internships are highly competitive. A paid internship usually requires planning. For the overwhelming majority of paid internships, you need to apply months in advance. If you want to participate in an internship over your summer vacation, you most likely need to apply for the position in the fall -- this is about a six to eight-month lead time.

It is highly unusual for students to apply for and receive a paid internship within a few weeks. If, for example, you are looking for an internship in the late fall for the early spring, it will be a challenge to find. In other words, do not wait.

For both paid and unpaid internships, you need to demonstrate you have something to offer your employer. The challenge is translating things you've done into skills an employer will value. For example, participating in team sports or campus groups provides valuable lessons for communicating as a team member. Think about the types of skills you need to effectively run a meeting, run for student government, or work on a group project.

Don't overlook the experiences your extra-curricular activities provide you. Consider the type of communication skills you developed, the type of promotional materials you might have created, or the presentations you delivered. Early in your career, these types of experiences are valuable opportunities to demonstrate your willingness to learn new things and participate in your community.

As a millennial, you face an interesting dilemma. Many people in the business world expect you to know everything there is to know about social media. Using social media for fun and using social media professionally are two completely different things.

Social media is a powerful tool for communication. As a college student or recent graduate, the thought of using social media professionally might not make much sense. Many adults, maybe even your professors, don't fully appreciate the power of social media. Yes, it is fun to create content to share with friends. Social media provide ways for us to participate in democracy and share with friends and family.

Social media are also a way for you to network and learn about job and internship opportunities. Remember applying for an internship is similar to applying for a job. If you want to obtain an internship where you can contribute and learn, you need to showcase your talents and skills on your LinkedIn profile.

The best way to do this is with a professional, complete LinkedIn profile. Although a complete profile will not get you a job, it will provide you the opportunity to showcase your skills and network with people.

It is now time to build your profile! Grab a cup of coffee or cappuccino, a pen, and some paper so you can start drafting your profile.

STEP 2: COMPLETE YOUR LINKED IN PROFILE

A good social media profile requires some creativity on your part. You must translate the experiences you do have into work-related needs. Descriptions, keywords, well-thought-out statements, a strong network, a professional profile picture, and media are all requirements for an All-Star Profile.

Each section of the profile serves a different purpose, and I'm going to discuss each one. Remember, the profile section is more than just filling in the blanks. The search algorithms index your terms, so I would encourage you to read each section's details and not jump ahead because it looks obvious.

LinkedIn organizes your resume in profile sections, including the following:

1. **Name** - Your first and last name
2. **Headline** - your current position described by keywords
3. **Location** - determined by zip code, but viewers of your profile will only see the city name
4. **Industry** – you will find choices located in the drop-down menu.
5. **Photo** - a professional headshot is best here
6. **Custom Background** - a 1400 x 1435 pixel image that represents your business or interests
7. **Contact Info** - this is only viewable to your connections
8. **Public Profile URL** - should contain your name and be as short as possible.

There are eight profile sections. Let's look at each of them.

First and last name

Type your name. If you have a nickname, consider whether or not you want to be known by this name. For example, if your name is Mary Colleen, but you are known as M.C., you must decide which name you will use in your profile. I tend to error on the side of your birth name. However, this is an individual decision. Select the name you are most comfortable with using professionally. Many people will search for your name, so keep it consistent.

Headline

The headline is an excellent opportunity to showcase who you are and the industry you either currently work or would like to. Your most recent job automatically populates the headline. However, you can and should change your headline. The algorithms use the terms in your headline, so choose your words carefully.

As a college student with little full-time job experiences, you can write something like this:

- Senior Finance major and President of Student Activities
- Division III Athlete Majoring in Sports Broadcasting
- Recent graduate of (your university) majoring in (your major)

You want to highlight what you are doing right now in as few words as possible. The algorithms will use the words in your headline to identify you. I can't stress enough how important the words you use influence the search engines. If you want people to find you, the words you choose for each section of your profile hold weight. Don't throw away any words.

Be deliberate. Take your time crafting your headline. I tell my students it is harder to write a few sentences briefly than to write an entire paragraph. Why? Because when you write deliberately, you need to identify the most impactful words. Those words are used in the algorithms so recruiters and hiring managers can find you.

Location

When you type in a zip code, it will populate a location. In some cases, it will provide for a more general location, such as the Metro New York area.

If you are looking for a job or internship near a major city, this is a good option because you will have more opportunities available to you. If you are more interested in working locally, be aware, you might be limited in the number of options. A smaller market can work to your advantage because small to medium-sized companies might have more flexibility, which means you could learn more than one area of the business.

Industry

What type of jobs interest you? If you are like most college students, you might not know what you want to do. Something to consider and ease your anxiety, remember your first job in the overwhelming majority of instances will not be your last job. Research indicates most individuals change careers (not jobs) at least five times over their working years.
Spend a little bit of time researching different industries - this is a crucial step to help you focus and identify keywords you can use for your headline and summary. Are you a Communication major? Are you interested in publishing and writing, broadcast, or corporate communication? Be specific.

Look for jobs you are interested in, and then identify the industry. LinkedIn lists over fifty different. A few examples include:

Accounting
Alternative Medicine
Banking
Biotechnology
Broadcast Media
Consumer Goods
Education
E-Learning
Entertainment
Marketing & Advertising
Music
Photography
Publishing

And the list goes on.

Take some time and think about what makes sense for your profile. I would not choose Education unless you are an Education major. Many students tend to use Education as their industry affiliation. It is a mistake many college students make when creating a profile. You think because you are attending college, you should identify Education as your industry. Identify the industry in which you want to work.

The industry you choose for your profile is one of those little LinkedIn secrets. It's not really a secret, but many people don't realize the industry you select for your profile affiliates you with others in the same industry. It is also how recruiters and hiring managers will find you. Aim toward the industry you would like to work in or obtain an internship. You can always update your industry later if you change your mind.

Don't panic if you are not 100% positive when you create your profile. Select the industry you are most confident and comfortable with using. The industry you would most like to affiliate with and work – that is most important.

Profile Photo

The importance of your profile photo cannot be understated. It is the first impression people will have you when they look at your LinkedIn profile.

I provide guidelines here so you can choose the best profile photo for your needs.

Remember: You are communicating about yourself non-verbally in your photograph. Your hairstyle, clothing, facial expressions, and background all speak to the viewer. This attention to deal requires planning.

Whether you like it or not, potential employers will make judgments about you based on your photograph. Are you honest? Credible? Hard-working? A team-player? No one, including you, makes these judgments to be mean. We use them to filter out information and make quick decisions about unfamiliar people, places, and situations.

Let's look at three photographs of the same person and identify what works and what doesn't work for a LinkedIn profile.

Please pay close attention to what the person is wearing, his/her facial expression, and the photograph's setting for each picture.

Before we review the photographs, let's identify different types of clothing choices. Clothing, hair, accessories, and the style of the picture are critical ways we communicate non-verbally.

Clothing & Accessories

Your choice of clothing is one of the most important decisions you will make for your profile photograph.

Most of us wake up every morning and choose what we are going to wear. Some of us spend more time and energy deciding than others, but every object you place on your body is a decision, a choice for how you want to present yourself to the world.

Some mornings you just roll out of bed and head to class still in your pajamas. Stop laughing. We both know you've done this at least one time during your college career. When you do this because you don't want to be late to class, it is understandable. However, what does it say about your time management?

When you decide to "get dressed up," what exactly does this mean? Typically it implies care taken to coordinating an outfit you feel comfortable and confident wearing. If you are an athlete, you might wear your team jersey to class. You do this because whether you realize it or not, you want others to know you are a member of or a fan of a team.

Clothing need not be expensive to look professional. There are typically four types of business dress. They include:

1. Business formal
2. Business professional
3. Business casual
4. Casual

Business Formal is most suitable if you want to work in law, are expected to meet regularly with executives, or otherwise hold a high-level position. Business formal is the highest level of professional dress.

For men, business formal includes a tailored one-, two-, or three-button suit in a solid, neutral color like black, gray, or navy. Ties and other accessories should be both modest in color and style – solid, brighter colors (a red tie, for example), or patterned muted neutrals (a navy plaid tie) – as well as high-end in quality. No novelty ties, such as sports team patterns. White, collared button-up shirts.

For women, business formal includes a well-cut pantsuit or skirt suit in a conservative, neutral color. Black, navy, or brown or all good choices. White button-ups with a collar. Closed-toe heels in a neutral color. Black, brown, and grey are acceptable. Accessories should be conservative—small studs rather than a chandelier or large hoop earrings. Wear hair in a traditional cut. Skirts are never shorter than two finger-widths above the knees.

2. *Business Professional* is step down from business formal. With professional business clothing, you still appear neat, conservative, and traditional. Business professional is also sometimes called "traditional business."

Business professional for men includes a one- or two-button suit. Suit colors should still be conservative, but you have slightly more leeway with the pattern. Pressed, lighter-colored dress pants worn with a sports jacket are appropriate. Ties should be traditional, but you can introduce colors and patterns. Shirts should be collared button-ups. Stick to blue, burgundy, or gray colors.

Business professional for women includes a suit or skirt, top, and jacket in a conservative, neutral color, such as black, brown, or navy. Collared button-up shirts may be any solid color—dark or nude-colored hosiery. Larger, more noticeable jewelry – as long as it's not distracting - is acceptable.

3. *Business Casual* is one of the more common dress codes in North America, allowing employees to add personality to their workwear without looking unprofessional. In a business casual setting, you can expect a lot more in color and accessories. The term "business casual" can mean different things to different organizations. Sometimes business casual can also be called

"executive casual."

For men, business casual includes colored, collared button-ups in any color. Conservative patterns such as checks or stripes are acceptable too, worn with or without a tie. Avoid novelty ties, and choose patterns like dots, stripes, or checks. Most colors are acceptable—pullovers and sweaters worn over a collared shirt. Choose solid, striped, or another conservatively patterned sweater. Dressy slacks, such as black dress pants or pressed khakis, are worn with or without a sports jacket in the summer.

For women, business casual includes business separates, rather than a full suit – a skirt worn with a cardigan or jacket—colored shirts and blouses, rather than mandatory collar button-downs. Choose solid colors or muted patterns like stripes or checks and avoid low-cut shirts or bright prints. Larger jewelry, such as a statement necklace or large cuff-style watch, can be worn.

4. *Casual office settings.* If you are fortunate enough to work in a casual office, the trick is to avoid getting too relaxed or creative with your dress. Remember, your co-workers make specific judgments regarding your capability based on your clothes, which may extend to employers as well.

For men, casual office clothing includes: pants and slacks, but never jeans. If jeans are permitted, dark-wash, straight-cut only. Crew-neck sweaters, collar polos, and pullovers are acceptable.

Not everyone will agree with this advice. Use your best judgment for your profile photograph.

Now that we have identified the different types of business attire let's look at three potential LinkedIn profile photos. What do you notice about the woman's clothing in example #1?

The clothing is very casual - a cropped t-shirt and jeans. Is this outfit appropriate for a job in a corporate office? The obvious answer is no.

Although her outfit is fashionable and perhaps entirely appropriate for an Instagram post, we must ask if this the right photograph for a professional LinkedIn profile, even for jobs where casual clothing would be allowed. It is

always best to dress conservatively (no midriffs, no selfies) when selecting a LinkedIn profile picture.

Selfies are not professional and should not be used for your LinkedIn profile photograph. You are better off using the self-timer on your phone if you plan to take your own photo.

Facial Expression

The next thing to consider is facial expressions. Facial expressions are one of the essential elements of your photograph next to your clothing.

What does her expression convey? Is this a person you would want to hire to work in your office? This expression screams, "I don't care what you think about me." If I were an employer looking for an intern, it might raise a red flag. Is this person a team player or self-focused?

A gentle smile is always a good choice for a profile photograph.

Background of Photograph

An easy element to overlook is the background. Look at photo #1. Can you identify the location? Is this an appropriate business-related background? Not at all. The photograph was taken in the bathroom. Not at all suitable for a LinkedIn profile image. There are so many better options for your picture!

You might be thinking that one is obvious! I know you know better. But, what about the picture of the same woman sitting on the steps?

This photo is more serious, no midriff is showing, and it is not a selfie. Would this photograph be appropriate for a LinkedIn profile? In most cases, I would say no.

While the photograph is artistic and beautiful, it does not reflect an open and friendly personality. The subject looks aloof and unfriendly. Additionally, the subject is wearing workout clothing. Not appropriate even for a business casual setting.

Remember, you have one chance to make a first impression on LinkedIn. The first thing a visitor to your profile will see is your photograph and your headline. Select a picture that will showcase you at your best. Wear what you would for a job interview in the industry you would like to work.

If, for example, you want to work in finance, it might be best to wear a suit for your profile photograph. There is an old saying, "dress for the job you want, not the job you have."

Gentlemen should wear a collared shirt regardless of industry. Some may choose a tie or a suit. While not necessary, it communicates your seriousness, openness, and understanding of the business climate.

Is a t-shirt ever appropriate? You need to use your best judgment. If you decide to wear a t-shirt, be sensitive to any logos or graphics on the t-shirt. A plain solid t-shirt could work, although I do not recommend it.

Let us examine the final photograph (#3) of SmileStyleSlay fashion blogger Samantha Rae.

What do you immediately notice about this photograph? She is smiling, dressed professionally (but not stuffy), and the background does not overwhelm. The lighting provides lightness and professionalism to the photo. Photo #3 is a professional photograph explicitly taken for her

LinkedIn profile, and I think it works for her.

When creating your profile photo, it is always best to plan what you will wear and identify a location to take the picture.

Notice I wrote, *create* your picture, and not take your picture because professional photographs are created. One of the striking differences between an amateur and a professional portrait is the attention to detail.

A few things to consider as you prepare for your profile photograph. Ask for help. If you can't afford to pay a professional photographer, you can work with a friend or family member who has a camera. Take many different photos in different locations with different lighting, so you have choices. Natural lighting works well if you can afford a studio portrait, and it always produces the best photos.

When choosing clothes, remember solid colors typically look best for profile photos because they do not distract from you. I prefer smiling for pictures. However, a more serious look could best represent your personality. Consider and practice your facial expressions in a mirror. I know this sounds odd, but it works. Trust me.

After you've planned your photoshoot and have your photos ask friends and family for advice on which picture, they like best. Sometimes we overlook essential details. It is also an excellent idea to ask people of different ages. It is not very likely someone your age is going to hire you for a job or internship. Hiring managers and recruiters will most likely be older than you and have different expectations. Make sure to ask parents, aunts, uncles, or a colleague.

Just remember: your profile photo should reflect your personality.

Banner Image

A custom background is also known as the banner image. An often-overlooked area of your profile is the banner or custom background. The area directly above your profile photo is valuable real estate, so don't forget to create a custom background.

Many individuals have no background, while others use the standard options provided by LinkedIn. Still, an All-Star profile should include a banner that highlights your accomplishments or something interesting about you.

You can create a banner in Canva for free. Canva is a graphics program you can use to create social media graphics. The platform provides a LinkedIn banner as an option.

One caveat is to use graphics, colors, and fonts carefully. Although it is easy to create a banner, you want to make sure you don't create a too busy banner. Less is always more with any design.

Suppose you have no experience with layout or design. In this case, use one of the built-in templates in Canva and customize it. It is better to use a template than to create a banner that looks too amateurish or sloppy.

You can choose to highlight your accomplishments, interests, awards, or any other visual images you believe will help you develop your digital brand on your banner. You can also keep it simple with a picture of campus or a skyline. Think of the banner as another way to brand yourself—a way to non-verbally communicate something positive about yourself.

Contact Information

You can manage the contact and personal information displayed in the introduction card on your profile by editing the Contact Info section.

Some details are only visible to your connections. You can choose what contact information you provide and who can view your email from your Settings & Privacy page.

Consider the best email. Are you going to use your college email address or a personal email? Do you want your contact information visible to the public or contacts only?

Public URL

Another often overlooked feature of LinkedIn is that you can customize your public profile URL. Custom public profile URLs are available on a first-come, first-served basis.

I highly suggest doing this if you are actively looking for a job or internship, and you have content on other social media platforms you would like to showcase. Of course, it might not be appropriate for all platforms and all of your accounts. Use your best judgment.

STEP 3: WRITE YOUR SUMMARY

In addition to your photo and custom banner, your profile summary is the place where you can shine! Leaving your summary profile blank or incomplete is a big mistake. Aside from your photo, the profile summary is one of the first things people see.

If a visitor to your site is not a first-level connection, LinkedIn allows them only to read the first 300 characters. Because of this limitation, take extra care when writing the summary.

The words you choose for your first few sentences might be the only thing a visitor to your site - a potential employer - reads. You will need to wordsmith. Being a skillful writer takes time. To help you through this part of the process, I have included a few examples to get you started.

Your summary statement reflects who you are, what you have accomplished, and any specific talents or skills you possess. Another way to think of the summary statement is as an elevator pitch. In the business world, the "elevator pitch" is what you would say to a potential customer or client to gain their interest in your product, service, or idea.

Imagine you are in an elevator with the person responsible for hiring you for your dream job. What would you say if you only had 60 seconds to persuade a potential employer to hire you or schedule an interview? That is tough to answer off the top of your head for most people.

If you need some help with writing more succinctly, I highly recommend William Zinnser's book On Writing Well. In it, he addresses the importance of choosing words well, not including unnecessary language, and taking the time needed to edit and refine your writing. The key to writing a strong summary is your ability to tell your own story using keywords and phrases to highlight your accomplishments.

Have you won any awards or worked on any projects? Have you volunteered for any social causes? What skills do you currently possess? Are you able to edit using Premiere Pro, PowerPoint, or Excel? Do you belong to any organizations? Are you involved on-campus? When writing your summary statement, focus on what you have done and what you can do.

Write your summary statement and then edit it. Edit. Edit. Edit. Good writing requires editing, and editing takes time. You will want to write multiple summary statements with different openings. Ask friends and family for feedback and suggestions.

Summary Statement Examples

1. Writer, editor, and content strategist with a knack for telling stories and a flair for detail. I blend storytelling and persuasion tactics to share your brand's message and get you new clients. I love working with fashion companies, emerging technology, and online learning platforms. My favorite brands are unconventional and full of personality.

2. My passion for creativity and constant learning is accompanied with the thrill of production. I'm the video editor who wants to edit not just get the job out the door. I enjoy compiling and splicing clips, color correcting, and animating motion graphics. I take pride in my work because editing is what I love to do.

3. I'm an honors Communication student with a record of academic success. As the former captain of the volleyball team and an active member of the Public Relations Student Society of America, I have been recognized for my leadership skills by faculty and classmates.

4. Enthusiastic, highly motivated Finance student with proven leadership capabilities who likes to take the initiative and seek out new challenges.

You get the idea! Write about what you love, what you are passionate about, what you can do, or what you would like to do. Some, but not all, people believe you should write in the first person. I think you need to feel comfortable with your summary statement.

Write a draft version now, then revisit it after you've complete the other sections of your profile so you can refine it.

STEP 4: COMPLETE WORK EXPERIENCE

Head over to the Experience section - this might feel a little intimidating if you have limited work experience. Do not panic. You should list your most recent positions.

When I talk to students about their work experience, they sigh or shrug because they have minimal work experience or none. Here is what you need to remember: your summer and part-time jobs can be valuable assets for your profile at this point in your career journey.

When you are completing the experience section, you need to get a little creative. I live in a small coastal shore community where summer jobs and part-time work is plentiful. While the jobs might be limited to stocking shelves or waitressing, it is possible to use these experiences for now to highlight the skills you do have.

You do this by thinking about all the things you need to do to perform your job. If you stock shelves, is there a process you follow? Did you receive training? Do you also work with customers if they need help? Are you able to use a particular software program? Are you fast? Accurate? A team player?

These qualities are essential to highlight so you can take the next step on your career journey. Each work experience you have is a valuable step toward an internship or job related to your chosen career.

Provide a title and add a job description.

To help you write the description, I've provided a few examples to get started. If your employer provided a job description, use it. If not, identify the skills you used to execute your job to help you write the description.

If the company appears in the drop-down once you start typing, click on it to ensure you get grouped with fellow employees under company searches.

Use a variety of keywords and terms in describing what you did in skill-based terms. For example, if you worked waitressing, did you exhibit a high level of customer service? Are you good under pressure? An excellent communicator? Can you work in a fast-paced environment?

Here are a few ways to think about the language you can use for your experience.

Job Description Examples

Job: Student Worker, English Department

Examples of Job Responsibilities for a Student Worker
- Assist with answering telephones, faxing, filing correspondence, running errands on campus, stuffing envelopes and making copies.
- Greet office guests, answer questions and direct to the proper individual(s).
- Data entry into a Microsoft Excel spreadsheet; database, etc.
- Make suggestions on how to streamline a process or task that is manual.

Example of Qualifications
- Complete tasks with minimal supervision.
- Learn new skills as necessary.
- Exhibit excellent communication skills, attention to detail, and solution-oriented.
- Comfortably operate Microsoft Office software.
- Support students, faculty, and administration in a positive professional manner.
- Uphold FERPA and other confidential matters.

Job: Waitress/Waiter

Example of Responsibilities (Waitress/Waiter)
- Greet and escort customers to their tables
- Present menu and provide detailed information when asked (e.g.

about portions, ingredients or potential food allergies)
- Prepare tables by setting up linens, silverware, and glasses
- Inform customers about the day's specials
- Offer menu recommendations upon request
- Up-sell additional products when appropriate
- • Take accurate food and drinks orders, using a POS ordering software, order slips or by memorization
- Communicate order details to the Kitchen Staff
- Serve food and drink orders

Job Requirements (Waitress/Waiter)
- Hands-on experience with cash register and ordering information system (e.g. Revel POS or Toast POS)
- Basic math skills
- Attentiveness and patience for customers
- Excellent presentation skills
- Strong organizational and multitasking skills, with the ability to perform well in a fast-paced environment
- Active listening and effective communication skills

Think about presenting your work experience to highlight what you did well and how you did it. Do not take part-time jobs, volunteer experiences for granted. They are essential early in your career.

STEP 5: STUDENT PROFILE SECTION

LinkedIn provides profile sections specifically designed for students. This area of the platform includes Courses, Projects, Certifications, and Organizations.

Take full advantage of this area of LinkedIn. It is a great place to showcase your college coursework, accomplishments, and awards.

Head to the profile section under accomplishments. You will find a list of categories you can add to your profile. As a college student or recent graduate, you will want to pay special attention to the following categories: courses, projects, honors & awards, test scores, languages, and organizations.

Courses

Minimally, you need to add relevant coursework to your profile. Early in your career, coursework can help you highlight and distinguish your areas of interest. Provide a brief description of the course. Only highlight courses where you excelled.

You have taken a lot of courses in college, which ones should you highlight? Any class where you excelled, and you can showcase the skills you gained. For example, have you taken any Media Production or Graphic Design classes? Do you know any software programs? Have you taken Creative Writing or Research classes? Those types of studies provide opportunities to showcase tangible skills you can use on the job.

A note of warning: do not overwhelm your profile with courses. Be selective and intentional. Consider whether the course relates to the industry where you would like to work. If so, how? Do not leave it up to the reader to figure it out. Do the work so your reader does not have to.

Another often overlooked type of coursework is online courses. Taking an online course requires organization and discipline. Many times, you are working independently and are required to manage online software programs. If it makes sense for you, add online courses where you excelled. Explain how the course helped you develop skills like time management and working independently.

Honors & Awards

Honors and awards are other areas where you can shine. Have you been featured in a newspaper, magazine, or online publication? If so, make sure to include the award or recognition. Honors and awards are an excellent place for you to showcase recognition for excellence or service.

Languages

If you are multilingual, you should highlight the languages you can speak. Do note if you are fluent in speaking and reading the language. Speaking more than one language can be incredibly valuable to a potential employer. Don't take your language skills for granted!

Organizations

Campus life is more than just taking college classes. The time you spend at college may also involve participation in a college activity. Have you participated in student government, student activities, or an athletic team?

Maybe you were inducted into an association like the National Honor Society or the Public Relations Student Society of America. This section of your profile is a valuable way to highlight experiences you have that might not be in your summary or work experience but relate to your future career.

TIP: If you are still in college and have time, consider joining a student organization related to your interests. Not only will it look good on your resume, but you will also meet people with similar interests. It is a great way to develop your networking skills while you are still in school. If you are involved in an organization, identify the roles you've held. Are you a member, or do you have a leadership position? Be sure to include how you were involved and what you accomplished.

Publications

Has anything you have written ever been published or featured by an outside source? Have you written a blog post that has gained considerable attention or is on a controversial topic? Have you contributed to anyone else's publication? Maybe you have worked with a professor on a research project. Be sure to add any publications to your profile.

Volunteer Experience & Causes

In many colleges across the country, students need to complete a service requirement. If you have volunteer experience or support a particular cause, you should include it on your profile. Think about what organizations you support that are related to your future career. Are you a strong advocate for any causes, local or national? Have you participated in any volunteer events in your community? If so, carefully write the descriptions for each entry, so it contains keywords from your profile.

Projects

College is a great time to develop project management skills. We have all worked on a team with classmates. Sometimes the experience is excellent and other times not so much. Think about projects you have worked on relevant to the skills required for a job you would like.

Projects include helping to organize an event or working on a service project. For example, working with Habitat for Humanity is a wonderful way to highlight experiences that might not fit your profile's traditional work experience section. Utilizing categories specifically designed for college students or recent graduates is another way to digitally brand yourself and connect with others from your alma mater. These connections will come in handy when you start asking for endorsements.

STEP 6: ADD A SKILLS SECTION

The skills section is the perfect way to showcase your talents, your abilities, and your strengths. LinkedIn allows you to add 50 skills to your profile.

You will want to use a combination of hard and soft skills. Keep in mind that while soft skills – like leadership, communication, and teamwork- are necessary and essential - employers like to see tangible skills, also called hard skills.

Hard skills are things like graphic design, video editing, scriptwriting, and project management. As a college student, you will have opportunities to build tangible skills in some of your courses. You will want to list your most important skills first and then feature your top 3 skills.

Once you add skills to your profile, you can then ask for endorsements.

STEP 7: ASK FOR ENDORSEMENTS

You will notice a hyperlink under each position that says, "Ask for recommendations." Recommendations are a great way to distinguish yourself. You can illustrate how well you performed through a colleague's narrative.

Often, you will need to request a recommendation. Do not merely send the generic message LinkedIn creates for you when asking a former supervisor or co-worker for a recommendation. It is always better to include specific projects you worked on so that your recommender can speak to the work you did.

I realize how uncomfortable it can be to ask for a recommendation. However, this should not prevent you from doing it. When thinking about who to ask, I suggest only asking people who can honestly speak to your abilities, attitude, and work ethic. If you only have one or two recommendations, you will want one, if not both, to be from a supervisor, mentor, or college professor with who you have worked closely.

The keyword here is that you worked closely with the person you are asking. It makes little sense to ask a professor who cannot specifically speak to your abilities. If you do not have anyone to ask right now, keep this in mind for the future.

Endorsements are an excellent way to network on the platform and emphasize your fabulousness!

STEP 8: ADD MEDIA

After you have optimized your profile, you will want to add media. To me, the media section is one of the most critical but often overlooked features of LinkedIn.

The media feature is a key differentiator for many students because it functions much like a digital portfolio. Please take full advantage of it.

Adding media to your profile is smart because you can highlight your best work in one place. LinkedIn provides the ability to add media to your profile (the featured media section), and you can add media to each position you have held. Use both sections.

You will want to add media to your profile that speaks to your strengths, such as writing assignments, presentations, a personal website, photographs, or video editing projects. You can also add news and magazine articles. Anyone in your network can access any media you share to your profile. This one feature is an excellent way for hiring managers, recruiters, and your connection to learn more about you and your skills.

You have worked hard in your courses, and you need to showcase what you have learned!

STEP 9: GROW YOUR NETWORK

Once you have the basics of LinkedIn complete, it is time to take your profile to the next level. A complete profile is essential, but it alone will not help you obtain your first job or internship.

Networking and nurturing relationships on LinkedIn are powerful ways to increase your chances of landing your dream job. The most important thing you can do once your profile is complete is to network. Building an All-Star profile but not networking is like buying an expensive car but never driving it. To make the most of the time spent on LinkedIn, you need a clear strategy.

Networking effectively is a skill you develop over time. It can be uncomfortable to reach out to people you've never met. Do it anyway. You would be surprised at how few students ever consider contacting people in their network. When you take the time to reach out to different people in an organization or industry where you want to work, it shows initiative.

A former student of mine took my advice when looking for internships. She found a company she wanted to work for and discovered an alumna work for the organization. She requested a connection, and a conversation started. To make a long story short, she now works full-time for the company and has moved halfway across the country. She could not be happier, and it all started because she was strategic in her networking strategy.

When it comes to networking on LinkedIn, there are two primary ways to build your network: 1) to get more meaningful connections and; 2) to nurture those relationships.

Before you begin building your network, you want to make sure you have a complete profile.

How to Build a Network

Since you are most likely just getting started on LinkedIn, you will want to connect with people you already know. Connect with friends, co-workers, alumni, as well as other students.

Many people only want to connect with people they already know. The hesitation is natural because it can be uncomfortable to reach out to people you don't know. However, to show up frequently in searches and see the maximum number of profiles, you will need to be bold in your networking strategy.

Reaching out to people you already know is simple. But this strategy will eventually work against you because of LinkedIn's algorithms.

Connecting and networking with someone you have never met requires a little more finesse and confidence. Here are a few suggestions to help you connect with people you do not know.

Personalized Connection Request

Yes, you will want to send a connection request – but not just any connection request --- you will want to craft a short but personal note about why you would like to connect or how you found them on LinkedIn.

Avoid using the template email generated by LinkedIn. Copied and pasted messages with no personality or customization read like spam. People tend to ignore them. You will have better success if you reach out to one person at a time with a customized message. You will appear more genuine and sincere.

Connection requests tailored to the person increase the likelihood the receiver will connect with you. While crafting individual connection requests takes a little more time, it is well worth it. As you are writing the request, consider what you might have in common with the other person. Is it an alumnus? Do you share mutual connections? Make sure to include that information in your request. Then, add why you would like to connect.

Research suggests generic requests tend to yield far fewer connections. If you have used LinkedIn for an extended period, you will get many connection requests. I am very selective in who I accept as a contact. I tend not to accept all connection requests – mostly because a generic email is used. While some suggest you should connect with as many people as possible, I think this is terrible advice. It will lead to many low-level connections with little value.

Ask for An Introduction

Another great way to grow your network is to ask your existing connections to introduce you to a person you would like to connect with if they already know that person.

For example, you can send a message to your connection that says something like this: "Hi Dr. Bob, I noticed that Mary is one of your contacts on LinkedIn. Would you mind introducing us? I would love to connect with her about a potential position available in her organization. I appreciate your time". If you use this strategy, be very specific as to why you want the introduction. The overwhelming majority of the time, your contact will introduce you – especially if you've given a reason why you would like the introduction.

Groups

Another great way to stand out to those you'd like to connect with is to find and join groups on LinkedIn. Why? Because they give you access to vast numbers of people who are all interested in the same topics you are. LinkedIn allows you to join up to 100 groups.

You will want to research various groups and join the ones populated by your target audience members. You can join groups related to your areas of interest, social causes, alumni, and profession-specific groups. It would be best if you looked for groups with many members and lots of activity.

Plan to be active in the group. Be selective, and join groups most interesting to you, so you will want to contribute to the community with thoughtful comments, likes, and shares.

LinkedIn is about relationship building and networking. Once you have connected with people, you will need to nurture the relationships -- this is the second component of networking.

To foster relationships on LinkedIn, you will want to like, thoughtfully comment, and even reshare posts your connections have shared.

In essence, you will want to be an active participant on the platform. Actively engaging with content and even creating content are powerful ways to develop professional relationships on LinkedIn.

Engage In The Newsfeed

Another way to connect and expand your network is to engage in the news feed. You can like, comment, and share the articles a person you admire shares or writes. Actively engage with their content and leave thoughtful posts about what you liked about what they wrote. After interacting with them for a while, then request to connect with them.

STEP 10: CHECK COMPLETENESS OF PROFILE

LinkedIn identifies All-Star profiles based on the completeness of the profile. An All-Star profile does not mean you have quality content, it just means you have completed each section of the profile. Aim for high-quality content on a complete profile.

Go through this checklist to confirm you took all the necessary steps to complete your profile:

- Full name
- Professional photograph
- Personalized Headline
- Summary with keywords
- Appropriate industry affiliation
- Media included on profile
- Complete work history with related media
- Skills identified with top 3 skills highlighted
- Customized URL
- Three recommendations on profile
- Joined and active with at least 1 group
- Frequent interactions with connections
- Frequent engagement in the newsfeed
- Custom background image (top of your profile)
- Student section includes projects, awards, and courses

Once your profile is complete, the time you spend on LinkedIn will vary from day today. If you are actively looking for an internship or a full-time position, you will want to spend time every day interacting with the newsfeed and in groups.

To stand out, you will want to consider posting content to LinkedIn. The posts you share can be in the form of blog posts, articles, edited videos, infographics, podcasts, or any type of media you think adds value to your connections. Just remember LinkedIn is a professional business communication platform. Anything you post needs to be related to the workplace or life-work balance.

How often you engage with your connections is a personal decision. Some might engage every day and others once a week. You will need to create a networking strategy that works for you.

CONCLUSION: ENJOY THE JOURNEY

Graduating from college is an exciting time. The world is yours. You have so many choices and options. Take time to think about the things you love, where you would like to live and the type of job you would like to have.

Take one small step at a time. It will not happen overnight, but it will happen if you put in the time. Use LinkedIn to help you on your journey. It is a fantastic tool if it is used right. Yet, it is only a tool. A complete profile is only the first step.

The magic of LinkedIn is the doors it can open. I have seen it happen with students time and time again. I know it works if you work it.

Never forget LinkedIn is a professional networking platform. You will have to network and nurture the relationships in your network. Sometimes, you will need to think outside of the box and reach out to people you do not know. Do not let fear hold you back from living your best life. You can do this!

Take the first step, then the second. Before you realize it, you will have a network – a community – and you WILL find the internship or job of your dreams.

The only thing stopping you now is you.

Made in the USA
Middletown, DE
09 October 2021